Turtle Snoots, Scutes, and Toots?

Fascinating Turtle Facts

Written by Jessica Lee Anderson • Photos by Bob Ferguson II

Paperback ISBN: 978-1-964078-33-5

To everyone who rescues turtles, and to one of my favorite turtles, Splash Thee Turtle. - JLA

To my son, Nathan - Whether swimming with Green Sea Turtles in Mexico or performing Bog Turtle surveys together in PA, you are my muse in my love of testudines. - BF

Note from the author: If you see a turtle crossing the road, first and foremost, stay safe! To help, encourage the turtle in the direction it was heading, never dragging it by the tail.

All photos taken by Bob Ferguson II apart from P. 24: Jessica Lee Anderson (Black-breasted leaf turtle), P. 30: Jessica Lee Anderson (Galápagos giant tortoise); P. 32: Michael Anderson and Mike Howlett

Names of species (current iNaturalist common names) clockwise from top left: Front cover: Eastern box turtle; Cover Page: Northern red-bellied cooter; Copyright: ; Dedication: Northern diamondback terrapin; P. 4: Green sea turtle, Ornate box turtle, Gopher tortoise; P. 5: Common snapping turtle, Florida softshell turtle, Eastern box turtle; P. 6: Northern diamondback terrapins; P. 7: Eastern box turtle, Gulf coast spiny softshell, Florida box turtle; P. 8: Marsh terrapin, Eastern box turtle, Bog turtle; P. 9: Wood turtle, Eastern box turtle, Florida box turtle; P. 10: Eastern painted turtle, Red-eared sliders, Peninsula cooter; P. 11: Wood turtle, Eastern box turtles; P. 12: Spotted turtle, Red-eared slider, Florida cooter; P. 13: Kemp's Ridley sea turtle, Green sea turtle, Kemp's Ridley sea turtle; P. 14: Northern map turtle, Common snapping turtle, Wood turtle; P. 15: Eastern musk turtle, Loggerhead musk turtle, Eastern musk turtle; P. 16: Mesoamerican slider, Blanding's turtle, Eastern painted turtle; P. 17: Eastern box turtle, Bog turtle, Eastern mud turtle; P. 18: Green sea turtle, Northern diamondback terrapin; P. 19: Eastern box turtles; P. 20: Northern diamondback terrapin, Blanding's turtle, Three-toed box turtle; P: 21: Ornate box turtle, Northern diamondback terrapin, Northern map turtle; P. 22: Alligator snapping turtle, Eastern box turtle (skull too), Northern diamondback terrapin; P. 23: Green sea turtle, Florida softshell turtle, Wood turtle; P. 24: Black-breasted leaf turtle, Eastern box turtle, Eastern river cooter; P. 25: Eastern box turtle, wood turtle, bog turtle; P. 26: Eastern hellbender and wood turtle, Spotted salamander and spotted turtle, Spectacled caiman and Mesoamerican slider; P. 27: Bog turtles, Marsh terrapins, Northern map turtles; P. 28: Common snapping turtle eggs, Painted turtle nesting, Common snapping turtle nesting; P. 29: Loggerhead sea turtle, Eastern mud turtle, Northern diamondback terrapin; P. 30: Red-bellied cooter and musk turtle, Galápagos giant tortoise, Common snapping turtle; P. 31: Green sea turtle, Desert tortoise, Chinese big-headed turtle; P. 32: Loggerhead sea turtle; Back cover: Wood turtle

This Book Belongs to:

_____

Differences Between Turtles and Tortoises

Turtles are reptiles, types of animals that are "cold-blooded" and usually have scales.

Tortoises are a type of turtle that tend to live on land (terrestrial). Tortoises have feet like elephants and walk on their toes. Not all turtles are tortoises. Certain turtle species live on land while other species live in watery environments like the ocean (aquatic). Some live on both land and water, like near ponds (semi-aquatic).

Turtle Snoots?

The word snoot is a variation of the word snout or nose. Like you, turtles have two nostrils (also called nares). Nostrils help turtles breathe as well as smell. Even turtle species that live in the water have a good sense of smell, important for finding food.

Turtle snoots can be a variety of shapes and sizes, and some even act like snorkels!

Super Shells

All turtle species have shells! Shells vary in size, shape, and color (even in the same species).

A turtle's shell is part of a turtle's skeleton! A turtle never leaves the shell, and the shell never falls off. The shell grows with the turtle.

Turtle Scutes?

Shells protect turtles. Some turtle species have scutes, or bony, plate-like scales that cover the outside of the shell (both the top and the bottom). Scutes act like shields. They're made of keratin, the same protein that forms hair and nails.

Not all turtle species have scutes! Some turtle species have a leathery skin that covers their shells instead.

Carapace

The top part of a turtle shell (the dorsal section) is called the carapace. The carapace is formed from the turtle's spine and ribs, and it is often made of bony plates that are covered in scutes. The carapace provides protection from predators like sharks and alligators.

Some turtles have a flat carapace that helps with speed while others have a protective dome shape.

Plastron

The bottom part of a turtle shell (ventral section) is called the plastron. The plastron acts like a protective breastplate (which is how it got the name). Like the carapace, the plastron is usually made of bony plates covered in scutes. It protects the turtle's belly and internal organs.

Some turtle species can be slow because their sturdy shell limits flexibility and range of motion.

9

"Cold-blooded"

Turtles do not stay a constant body temperature the way mammals and birds do. They regulate temperature by changing their environment, which is why they're called "cold-blooded" (though biologists will use technical terms like ectothermic or poikilothermic). Turtles often bask in the sunshine to warm up.

The carapace holds heat inside to allow turtles to maintain the necessary body temperature—even in cold water.

Basking Benefits

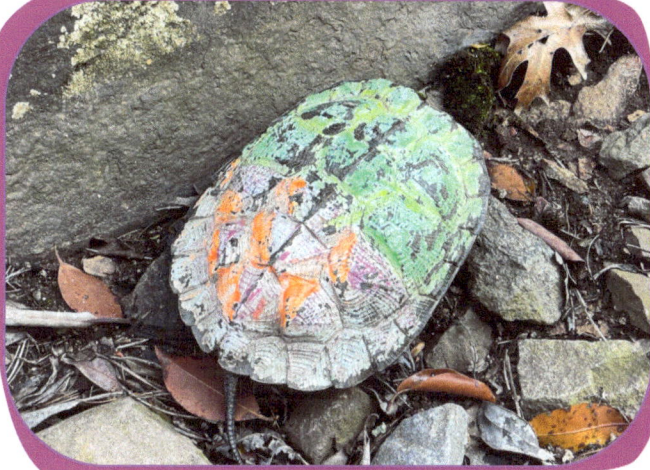

Besides getting to the right temperature, basking has other benefits. Sunshine helps turtles get Vitamin D, which is important for healthy shells and bones. While painting turtles might seem cute, the paint blocks this process and can cause the turtle to get sick and even die.

Basking can help a turtle dry out, preventing fungal infections. Basking also reduces parasites and promotes wound healing, plus digestion.

At the Surface

Turtles swim to the surface of water to breathe as they need oxygen.

Some turtles will bask at the water's surface to get to the right temperature. They'll also move to an area of water that is a preferred temperature.

Cold-Stunned?

If the water rapidly cools, sea turtles can become weak and stop swimming. Cold-stunned turtles will float at the surface or wash up on the shore. Wildlife authorities help rehabilitate cold-stunned sea turtles.

Butt Breathing?

The cloaca is a tube at the base of a turtle's tail that gets rid of waste and is part of the reproductive system.

Turtles technically have a cloaca instead of a butt. Certain freshwater species have a special adaptation—they can draw water through the cloaca into sac-like organs called bursae that act like aquatic lungs. Cloacal respiration helps a turtle survive in environments where it is hard to breathe air, like rapid rivers or frozen ponds.

Turtle Toots?

Just like people, turtles toot! Turtles fart after gas builds up when they swallow air while eating or when digesting food. If turtles can't toot, the extra gas can keep them from diving or staying underwater.

Some turtle species scare away predators with musk, a stinky form of defense from scent glands.

Camouflage

Plants can sometimes get stuck on turtles, especially in aquatic environments.

Many turtle species have camouflage adaptations that help them survive—they blend into their environment to hide from predators and to ambush prey (depending on species). Algae will sometimes grow on the shells of some turtles, acting like camouflage.

Colors and Patterns

Colors and patterns can help turtles camouflage in their native habitat. Many types of turtles are shades of green, dark yellow, gray, brown, or black. Several species have bright markings (especially on their necks) that attract mates.

Countershading

Certain turtles have a form of camouflage called countershading —this means they are lighter on the bottom than the top part of their shell. This helps them go unseen as they hide from predators or hunt.

When viewed from above, the turtle's darker back can be hard to see in the water. When viewed from underneath, the lighter colored ventral side blends in with the bright, watery surface

Color Changing

As many species age, their colors or patterns may change. Color changes are based on the environment in which the turtle lives. Diet and health can affect a turtle's coloration as well.

Many species will shed their skin and the scutes on their shells as they grow.

Hide and Seek

Turtles are experts at hiding among rocks, plants, mud, sand, and more. Hiding spots protect turtles and make them feel safe if they sense danger.

Retract!

Certain species tuck their heads straight back into the shell, while others retract their heads sideways.

When many species of turtles and tortoises sense danger, they have the ability to retract their heads (and even limbs in some cases) safely inside their shield-like shells. This offers protection and can help turtles hunt.

Beaks

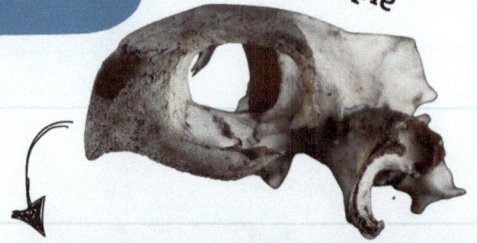

Turtles don't have teeth—they have beaks like birds. Their beaks have different adaptations depending on their diet, like crushing plates or saw-like serrations. Some turtles eat plants (herbivores), plants and animals (omnivores), or animals (carnivores).

Feet and Flippers

Instead of feet, sea turtles have flippers that help them swim. Aquatic turtles often have webbed feet that aid in speedy swims. Semi-aquatic and terrestrial turtles have more defined claws for digging. All turtle types can swim if necessary.

Excellent Eyes

Turtles can see well, even underwater! Given the placement of eyes on either side of their head, turtles have a good field of vision. A membrane protects their eyes.

Researchers have found that turtles see in color. They're extra sensitive to shades of red!

Hearing

Turtles don't have external ear parts like humans. They have tympanic membranes, or eardrums, on either side of their head covered by skin. Turtles can hear better underwater!

Habitat Overlap

Turtles share the same habitat with many different kinds of species, including salamanders and even predators such as caimans. Turtles will sometimes hitch a ride or bask on the back of predators!

Social Behaviors?

Turtles tend to be solitary, though they will hang out when courting, resting, basking, or nesting.

Nesting

All turtle species reproduce by laying eggs on land. Aquatic species will swim ashore to dig a nest, deposit eggs, and then cover the nest before returning to the water. Some turtle species lay over 100 eggs! Temperature determines if the eggs will be male or female. If walking at the beach at night, avoid flashlights as bright lights can disorient nesting turtles.

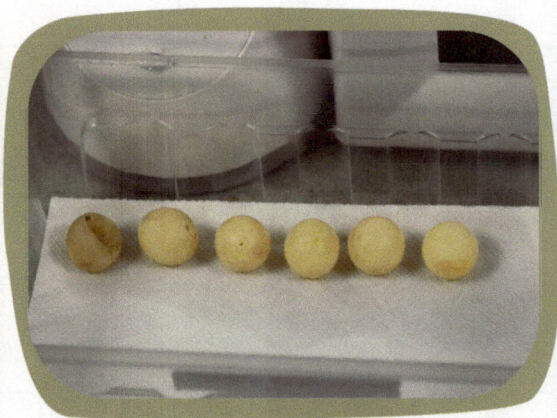

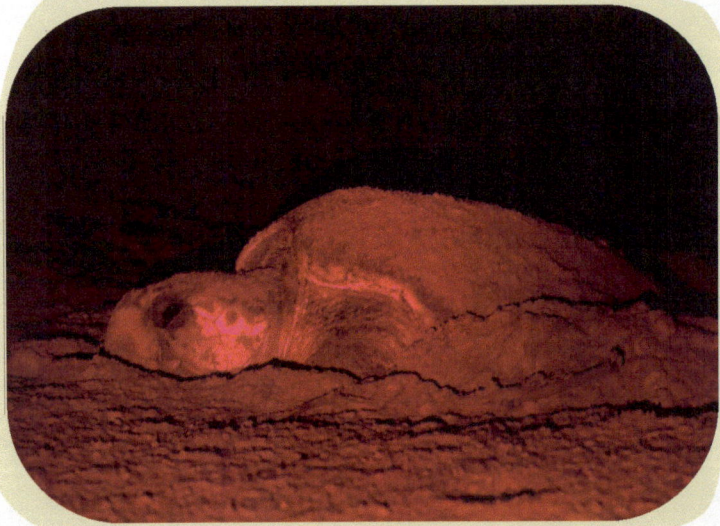

Hatchlings

Turtles will hatch in about two to four months. This will often depend on the species, temperature, and the depth of the nest. Babies will use an "egg tooth" to poke a hole in the egg, a process called pipping.

Babies will hatch out of the egg at their own speed, usually a couple of days later. (The "egg tooth" falls off soon after.)

Range in Size and Age

There are over 350 species of turtles in the world! Turtles vary in size and weight depending on the species and their age. Some species have long lifespans and can live over 150 years!

Fascinating Turtles

Turtles can be found in much of the ocean and on every continent except Antarctica.

Turtles can survive injuries and harsh conditions, though many species are at risk of disappearing from Earth (endangered). Scientists are continuing to learn more about these fascinating reptiles and how to protect them. They are important to healthy ecosystems!

Jessica Lee Anderson is an award-winning author of over 75 books for young readers. Jessica loves exploring the outdoors with her husband, Michael, and their daughter, Ava! Jessica admires many turtles at ponds near her home in Austin, Texas. You can learn more about Jessica by visiting www.jessicaleeanderson.com.

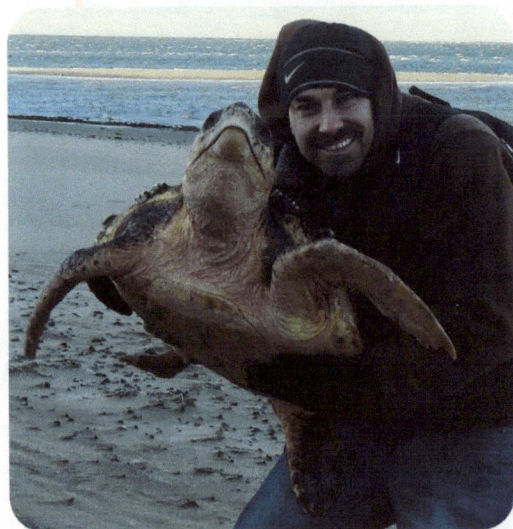

Bob is a naturalist with a compulsion to be outdoors. Wildlife conservation through entertainment, education, fundraising, and fieldwork is his mission and purpose in life. His organization, Fascinature, has donated six figures to saving land in the world's most biodiverse spaces. He even has a frog named after him! You can find him on Instagram @bob_ferguson_fascinature or sign up for his newsletter at fascinature.live.

Check out these other books!

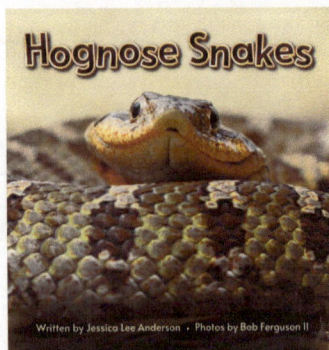

Hognose Snakes

Written by Jessica Lee Anderson • Photos by Bob Ferguson II

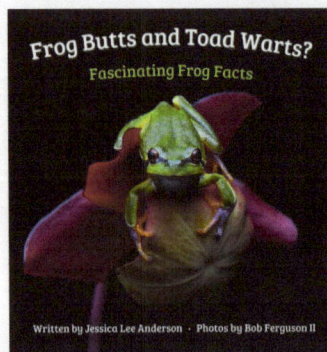

Frog Butts and Toad Warts?
Fascinating Frog Facts

Written by Jessica Lee Anderson • Photos by Bob Ferguson II

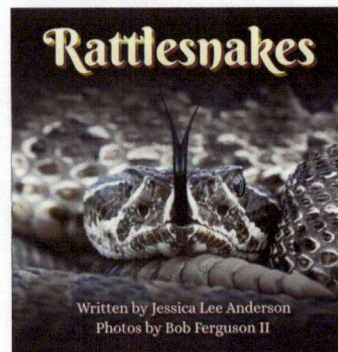

Rattlesnakes

Written by Jessica Lee Anderson
Photos by Bob Ferguson II

www.ingramcontent.com/pod-product-compliance
Lightning Source LLC
Chambersburg PA
CBHW061146030426
42335CB00002B/117